W9-BDT-376

SEEING RED

THE TRUE STORY OF
BLOOD

TANYA LLOYD KYI

ILLUSTRATED BY STEVE ROLSTON

annick press
toronto + new york + vancouver

Text © 2012 Tanya Lloyd Kyi
Illustrations © 2012 Steve Rolston

Edited by Linda Pruessen
Copyedited by Tanya Trafford
Proofread by Elizabeth McLean
Cover and interior design by Marijke Friesen
Cover illustration by Steve Rolston
Color assists by Dacosta!

Annick Press Ltd.

All rights reserved. No part of this work covered by the copyrights hereon may be reproduced or used in any form or by any means—graphic, electronic, or mechanical—without prior written permission of the publisher.

We acknowledge the support of the Canada Council for the Arts, the Ontario Arts Council, and the Government of Canada through the Canada Book Fund (CBF) for our publishing activities.

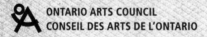

Cataloguing in Publication

Kyi, Tanya Lloyd, 1973–
    Seeing red : the true story of blood / Tanya Lloyd Kyi ; illustrated by Steve Rolston.

Includes bibliographical references and index.
ISBN 978-1-55451-385-7 (bound).—ISBN 978-1-55451-384-0 (pbk.)

    1. Blood—Juvenile literature. I. Rolston, Steve II. Title.

QP91.K95 2012   j612.1'1   C2011-906965-2

Printed and bound in Canada

Published in the U.S.A. by   Distributed in Canada by   Distributed in the U.S.A. by
Annick Press (U.S.) Ltd.   Firefly Books Ltd.   Firefly Books (U.S.) Inc.
                     66 Leek Crescent   P.O. Box 1338
                     Richmond Hill, ON   Ellicott Station
                     L4B 1H1   Buffalo, NY 14205

Visit our website at www.annickpress.com
Visit Tanya Lloyd Kyi at www.tanyalloydkyi.com
Visit Steve Rolston at www.steverolston.com

FOR MIN, WHO PUTS UP WITH
ALL MY OBSESSIONS AND ONLY
OCCASIONALLY SEES RED.
— T.L.K.

CONTENTS

INTRODUCTION
THE BLOODY FACTS 1

CHAPTER 1
BLOOD AND RITUAL 13

CHAPTER 2
RITES OF PASSAGE 31

CHAPTER 3
SIPS AND SUPPERS 47

CHAPTER 4
TIES THAT BIND 67

CHAPTER 5
READING THE BLOOD 91

CONCLUSION
A TASTE FOR BLOOD 105

FURTHER READING 112

SELECTED SOURCES 113

INDEX 116

ABOUT THE AUTHOR 120

ABOUT THE ILLUSTRATOR 121

OUCH! PAPER CUT!

de towa
e castle
dark gh
as blood.
of Drac

INTRODUCTION
THE BLOODY FACTS

BLOOD PACTS AND SACRIFICES. Blood brothers and blue bloods. Bloodletting and spatter patterns. The idea of blood flows through human culture the same way the real stuff flows through our veins. In almost every religion, there are blood sacrifices or blood rites. In almost every culture, there are rules for whether or not to eat blood, and how. There are blood ties, blood oaths, and countless blood-soaked legends.

Why was blood so important to our ancestors, and why does it retain such emotional power today? Most of us can't think of blood without shuddering slightly and hearing the faint flap of vampire wings. Why such revulsion over something so physically vital?

Well, there are as many opinions on that as there are blood types. But before we explore various cultures and their unique rites and taboos, we need to understand exactly how humans learned about what blood is, and what it does.

BLOOD BASICS

Today, the average grade four student probably understands more about blood than the world's most educated doctor did 500 years ago. Back then, blood was seen as one of many important but mysterious bodily fluids—something doctors tried to measure and regulate.

Here are some of the things people knew about blood in the year 1500:

- ☠ It pulses through your entire body.
- ☠ Upon death, it stops flowing.
- ☠ Bright red blood is different somehow from red-blue blood.

Here are some of the things people *thought* they knew about blood:

- ☠ It's produced by the liver.
- ☠ It carries emotions and ideas from the heart.
- ☠ Too much of it causes illness.

It took a long time—a seriously long time—for scientists to figure out what blood actually did. In the 13th century, a doctor working in Egypt noticed that the wall between the right side of the heart and the left was solid, which meant that blood couldn't pass through. He decided that blood must travel from the heart's right side to the lungs. Only then would it return to the left side, ready to be pumped through the body.

TRY TO AVOID THE POINTY END NEXT TIME.

THROUGH GALEN'S EYES

For thousands of years, Claudius Galen was considered the absolute authority on blood. He was born in 129 CE in what is now Turkey, traveled and studied extensively throughout the Mediterranean, and eventually moved to Rome to serve as a doctor for the gladiators.

At the time, it was against the law to examine dead human bodies, but Galen believed it was important to understand every detail of anatomy. He analyzed the bodies of apes and goats, dogs and pigs, inside and out. These scientific dissections taught him that blood flowed through the body. But why? In addition to his work as a doctor, Galen was a philosopher, searching for answers about life and the human spirit. He decided that circulating blood must be responsible for carrying a person's individual traits and characteristics.

In the average human body, there are enough blood vessels to wrap around the earth twice—with plenty left over. If you live to be 80, your heart will have pumped an amount of blood equal to the water in about 85 Olympic-sized swimming pools.

This guy was on to something! Unfortunately, his knowledge didn't spread outside the Arab world.

In the mid-1500s, a scholar and scientist named Michael Servetus was the first European to suggest the same thing. Unfortunately, he recorded his findings in a religious book instead of a medical one, and not too many people read it. When Servetus disagreed with the church on some major religious issues, he was burned at the stake. People's understanding of blood didn't get very far ...

In 1628, an English doctor named William Harvey finally outlined the circulatory system—the way the heart pumped blood through the arteries, and how the blood then completed a circuit through the body and returned to the heart. He said—and this was a shocker—that the liver was *not* the origin of blood.

A lot of other doctors refused to believe him, and even those who agreed didn't always admit it in public. After all, to do so would have meant casting aside thousands of years of medical knowledge.

BLOOD SUCKERS

nstead of continuing Harvey's research, or using it to develop new treatments for illness and disease, most of the world's doctors went right on using techniques perfected in ancient Egypt, Greece, and Rome.

Feeling sickly? Flushed and feverish? Sore throat and pounding head? Step right up. The doctors of past centuries had the cure for what ailed you. Once they extracted a cup or two of your blood, you'd feel much better. Really!

Well ... probably not.

Ancient Greeks believed that the human body contained four fluids, called "humors." Human health and happiness depended on keeping each fluid at its proper level.

☠ Is your friend stressed out? There's too much yellow bile in his system.

☠ Flushed with fever? Too much blood!

☠ A listless child? Poor thing has an excess of phlegm.

☠ Feeling blue? It's a case of copious black bile, obviously.

These ideas spread from Greece to Rome and the rest of Europe, and throughout the Middle East. In all of those places, one of the preferred medical treatments was the draining of blood. And people around the world continued the practice right up until the 1800s.

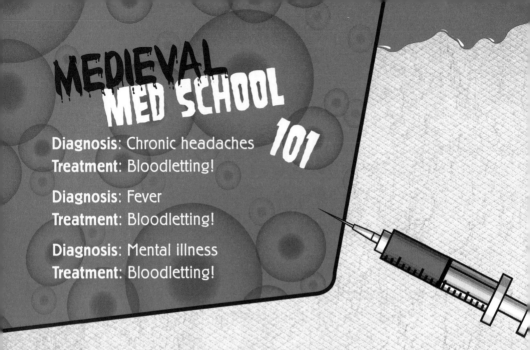

MEDIEVAL MED SCHOOL 101

Diagnosis: Chronic headaches
Treatment: Bloodletting!

Diagnosis: Fever
Treatment: Bloodletting!

Diagnosis: Mental illness
Treatment: Bloodletting!

DRIP, DROP

Bloodletting was all the rage in medical circles for more than 2000 years. Ancient pharaohs built pyramids. Gutenberg invented the first printing press. Alfred Nobel created dynamite. Engineers constructed the first railroads across North America. And all throughout that time, doctors everywhere were bleeding their patients.

There were, however, a few minor differences in technique. In Europe, doctors bled from the side of the body where the problem was located. In the Middle East, physicians chose the opposite

Leeches

side. Methods varied, too. Patients who were bled in England watched the fluid drain from a slice in their vein. In France, leeches were preferred. A few hungry bloodsuckers placed on the skin, and soon all that bad blood would be gone.

All of these bloodletting methods did have one thing in common: they were equally useless. If you were cured because of bloodletting, you would have healed anyway—and faster—without treatment.

Unfortunately, things didn't begin to change until the early 1800s. That's when a few scientists made some key discoveries:

☠️ Trés terrible! A French doctor started keeping detailed medical records (a startling new idea at the time). Eventually, these records began to show a pattern: blood-letting sucked.

☠️ Ooh la la! There are micro-scopic creatures crawling around in pus! Several scientists, including French chemist and microbiologist Louis Pasteur, helped prove that germs—not excess blood—made people sick.

MEDICAL RECORD
PATIENT A
TREATMENT:
BLOODLETTING
OUTCOME:
DEATH

MEDICAL RECORD
PATIENT B
TREATMENT:
BLOODLETTING
OUTCOME:
DEATH

MEDICAL RECORD
PATIENT D
TREATMENT:
BLOODLETTING
OUTCOME:
DEATH

So, that was that. Bloodletting was bad. Blood was good. It was indeed a key to life, just as Galen had thought way back in the second century.

In 1833, France imported 41.5 million leeches.

The Twilight series of vampire novels by Stephenie Meyer has sold more than 100 million copies and has been published in more than 35 languages.

It turned out that blood was much more important than yellow bile (whatever that is). It took air from the lungs and circulated it throughout the body, carrying oxygen to the muscles and the brain. Blood allowed the body to move and function.

Everything was explained. There was no more need to wonder. The End.

Or ... was it?

Well, first of all, many more scientific discoveries were made. Types of blood, and parts of blood, and uses for blood. (We'll get to all that later!) Those ideas continued to keep scientists busy for quite a while—right up until today, in fact.

Beyond science, though, there were other things that kept people wondering. For example: Was blood sacred? Did its relationship to life mean it had some connection to God? How did blood mark the border between childhood and adulthood? Was it safe to eat blood? Was it gross? How did blood tie families together? And when blood spilled from the body, as the result of a crime or an accident, what stories could it tell?

Around the world, many traditional cultures maintain their own ways of viewing blood—as a life force, as a symbol, even as a magical substance. And western culture has its own myths and ideas. If we didn't retain some mystical fascination with blood, we wouldn't watch so many vampire movies, or slow down to stare at car accidents.

BLOOD CULTURE

We often assume that the world's cultures are built around shared geography and history. Mountain-slope farmers in Tibet and commercial fishers in Portugal have different myths and legends because their people have evolved to survive in different climates and have lived through different experiences. Is it any wonder that each culture or society has its own things to explain and to reveal through art and storytelling?

Some anthropologists believe that culture has roots in the human body, as well. Ancient people must have found the beating of their own hearts just as fascinating as the path of the local river, or the height of the neighboring mountains.

In the same way that societies have developed elaborate myths to explain the creation of the world or the details of the landscape, people have come up with explanations for the workings of their own bodies.

Blood is a symbol in countless early creation myths. In various parts of the world, human beings were said to be born from the blood of the moon or from the spilled blood of a wounded god. In ancient Norse stories, humans were made of wood until the god Lodur gave them the blood of life.

In different parts of the world, blood is cleansing, or polluting. Blood is a symbol of weakness, or a symbol of strength. It's a source of great power—and great danger.

For many, blood is all of these things at the same time. That's because even in the ancient past, and even in diverse parts of the globe, people have understood one thing: blood is a basis of human existence. It plays a role in life, and a role in death. What substance could be more fascinating?

CHAPTER 1
BLOOD AND RITUAL

ANCIENT GODS were a demanding bunch. Offerings! More offerings! Keep those gifts coming! On special occasions, they insisted on the best. Not a mere handful of grain or a glass of water. No—they craved sacrifice. All over the world, from ancient Egypt to northern Europe, from North America to Australia, early peoples offered crops, wine, sheep—even children!—to please their gods.

Let's say you lived in Central America or southern Mexico ... oh, about 2000 years ago. You knew the gods wouldn't be satisfied with the offering of just a pig or a wild animal. They were thirsting for something better: human blood.

And not just the blood of any human, either.

The Maya people believed that their royal families were directly descended from the gods. So the best offering of all—the substance that would satisfy the deities and bring nourishment to the earth—was royal blood.

A Maya king or queen needed a good supply of the red stuff! To help their farmers bring in good harvests, and ensure their warriors won battles, Maya nobles ritually bled themselves. Their holy blood gave strength to the land and the people.

Today, historians think that this excess of blood loss might have given the rulers hallucinations, strong enough to make it seem like they were communicating with the gods themselves.

I'M JUST NOT FEELING THE WHOLE BLOODLETTING THING TODAY.

How does a queen offer her divine blood? One ancient carving shows a Maya ruler running a rope of thorns through her tongue. Ouch!

14

Bleed yourself for every battle? Donate blood before each harvest? It loses its appeal after a while! Maybe that's what the royals were thinking when they came up with a new way to satisfy their gods: bleeding *enemy* rulers. Capturing members of other noble families and slaughtering them became a favorite Maya war game. Sacrificing a few ordinary warriors never hurt either.

But there were a few problems with all of these bloody strategies. First, it was hard to wage war when your king and queen were delirious. Also, capturing and killing royal families tended to rid the world of experienced leaders. Finally, the gods didn't always listen. Sometimes crops failed, rains didn't fall, and armies lost battles. By the eighth century, the Maya civilization was in dire straits, with people fleeing war and famine and heading to the jungles.

SUN GODS AND SACRIFICE

n 1500, the Aztecs ruled the world—or at least central Mexico. In the stunning island capital of Tenochtitlan, they delighted in painting, dancing, and sculpture. They planted enormous flower gardens and studied the stars. And in between those civilized pursuits, they performed sacrifices to the gods—a LOT of sacrifices.

In one 16-year period, a king ordered 20,000 enemy warriors killed. And the people obeyed, accepting that the gods must be thirsty. The Aztecs believed that their ancestors had made a deal with the gods way back in the ancient past. To create the world, the gods had given their own blood. They'd formed the human race from their own divine bodies.

The Aztecs owed them one. Or 20,000.

To repay the gods, and to ensure the sun would keep rising and the corn would keep growing, the Aztecs believed they owed a constant debt of human sacrifice.

It wasn't a good time to be an enemy warrior.

💀 Were you captured during rites to Huitzilopochtli, god of war? Priests might slice into your chest, rip out your beating heart, and hold it toward the sun.

💀 Were you meant as a gift for the fire god, Huehueteotl? First you'd be burned *almost* to death before losing your heart.

💀 Maybe you were to be sacrificed to Tezcatlipoca, god of night. In that case, you'd be tied up while a group of Aztec warriors ripped you to pieces in a mock battle.

Today, everyone remembers the Aztecs for their gruesome rites. But they weren't the first to practice human sacrifice, or the last. In far distant corners of the earth, priests in other cultures were performing their own bloody rituals.

GIMME YOUR HEARTS!

TURKISH DELIGHT, ANYONE?

Ten thousand years ago, in the fields of what is now Turkey, there stood a wooden shack housing 90 human skulls and several skeletons. Oh, and a stone altar so drenched in blood that traces remain today.

What exactly were the farmers doing after their days in the fields? A flint knife was found among the remains, and there was a lot of animal blood on that stone, so archaeologists are guessing at some sort of sacrifice. But there was human blood, too. Were people sacrificed? Or bled after death? All historians know for sure is that what at first seemed like the remains of an ordinary little farming village turned out to be a strange and complicated place.

Other parts of Europe share similarly mysterious pasts. About 2300 years ago in northern France, the Gauls believed they were the descendants of the gods of the underworld. They supported this belief with rites and rituals that would have left even the strongest enemies shaking in their Greek or Roman robes.

Deep in a mud and wood temple lay an inner room, where only priests were allowed to be. There, the Gauls sacrificed animals caught in the wild. Later, they moved on to farm animals. And sometimes . . . well, sometimes only a human would do. Like the Maya and the Aztec people on the other side of the world, the Gauls sacrificed the bodies of their enemies.

At one ancient temple, archaeologists have found the bones of about a thousand enemy warriors, their weapons and armor piled nearby. Before burning these bones, the priests crushed them to expose the marrow, the bloody tissue in the center.

Why the marrow? The underworld gods were thought to crave human souls, and the Gauls, like many other early civilizations, believed a person's soul lived in the blood.

THAT TAKES GALL

If you were a Gaul warrior, here's how you'd celebrate a victory:

💀 Cut off all your enemies' heads.

💀 String the heads together and use them as a necklace for your horse.

💀 Sing a victory song.

💀 Nail a few heads to the doorway of your house, like hunting trophies.

If you'd won an extra-impressive victory over a particularly dangerous foe, you might want a special souvenir. In that case, you'd embalm an enemy head in cedar oil and stash it away in a cedar chest. You could show all your friends the next time they stopped by!

THAT'S SOME FUNKY SOUL

The whole blood/soul connection makes sense, if you think about it. When people are alive, blood pounds through their arteries. The veins on their arms show a purplish hue. Their heartbeats pulse in their wrists.

When death comes, all of this stops. Today, we know that when the heart stops beating, the blood stops flowing and begins to pool in the lower parts of the body. But they didn't know that 2000 years ago. They knew that two things happened at death: blood disappeared from the veins, leaving them translucent, and consciousness disappeared from the body. If the mind stopped working and the blood disappeared at the same time, the soul must reside *in* the blood. Right?

Burning bones was actually very practical—not necessarily because it appeased the gods, but because it freaked out potential enemies. After all, would you attack a fortress if smoke from human bodies was spiraling into the air?

Is it any wonder people made that connection? After all, the soul is a mysterious thing. Even today, no one knows for sure whether it exists, or where it might reside.

In the book of Genesis, the Bible tells believers that blood is life. Both Christians and Jews believe that God told Noah not to eat flesh that contained an animal's blood and soul. Like the ancient Gauls, early Jews and Christians made a blood/soul connection. So did the Romans. The poet Virgil called blood the *purpurea anima*, or the "purple soul."

To all of these people, blood held mysteries—mysteries that somehow formed the basis of human life, and death.

TAKE IT ON FAITH

Are you feeling relieved that you didn't live in the time of the Aztecs, or the Gauls? Not so fast! Blood is still a big part of religious rites today.

In southern India, the shamans of the Kaniyan people perform in an annual celebration to worship the god Sudalai, a deity who oversees evil spirits and who, without sacrifices,

According to the Jewish story of Passover, God instructed the Israelites to mark their doors with lamb's blood. Then the angel of death, sent to kill every first-born son in Egypt, skipped or "passed over" those homes marked by the sacrificial blood.

would disrupt the lives of the living. On the central day of the festival, worshipers pile offerings on a large platter—bananas, betel, coconut, and incense. A shaman stands over the offering and slices his wrist until blood flows freely over the items below.

In many ancient rituals, people believed that blood sacrifices were symbolically consumed by the gods. In this instance, however, the symbolic becomes real. Certain people in the Kaniyan tribe are believed to be possessed by the spirit of Sudalai. When these individuals eat the sacrificial food, mixed with the shaman's blood, it is as if the god has eaten the offering directly.

THE FLESH QUESTION

Worshipers of Sudalai feed their god with human blood. Christians feed themselves with their god's blood. The Bible says that Jesus, the son of God, broke bread and said: "Take and eat; this is my body." Then he lifted his wineglass and said, "For this is my blood…shed for many for the remission of sins."

Christians believe that Jesus sacrificed his body and his blood so that all believers could have their sins forgiven. In churches all over the world, modern Christians still regularly celebrate Communion—a ceremony in honor of Jesus' last meal. They eat bread (representing flesh) and drink wine or grape juice (representing blood) to commemorate his sacrifice.

Here's the big question: If Jesus said, "This is my flesh," does that mean the bread *becomes* his flesh? Are people eating something that has mysteriously turned into flesh? Are they drinking wine that has transformed into blood? Some Christians—the Roman Catholic Church, for example—say yes. When believers sip from the Communion cup, they are drinking the real blood of Jesus. Other churches, such as the Presbyterian, say no. The wine and the bread are only symbols.

IS THAT REALLY WINE?

PASS THE TISSUE, PLEASE

The Communion table is not the only place blood shows up in Christianity. There's the crucifixion, when Jesus was killed and his blood became a sacrifice to God—a sacred fluid that washed away the sins of the world.

And what about the stranger stuff? Like when a statue of the Virgin Mary, mother of Jesus, starts shedding tears of blood?

There have been plenty of reports of crying Madonnas. Maybe there's political or religious trouble in the country, and people start looking for guidance, or even a miracle. All of a sudden someone notices that the statue of the Virgin Mary in the town plaza just happens to be weeping blood.

It's occurred in California, in Japan, in Rome—all over the world.

The Catholic Church is quite careful about confirming these "miracles." When something like this occurs, church officials arrive like crime scene investigators. In 1995, they proved that a weeping statue in Italy was dripping male, not female, blood. The statue's owner—a man—refused to give a blood sample. In 2008, investigators matched the blood of another weeping statue to that of the church janitor.

RELIGION V.S. ROOSTERS

Cuban-American followers of the Santeria religious group have caused ongoing controversy in Florida by sacrificing animals. One rite calls for burying the blood of three roosters along with corn, bananas, candy, and rum. To animal rights activists, the slaughter of roosters and other animals is barbaric. Others argue that all people should enjoy religious freedom, even if their religion involves killing animals. Who's right? One case went to the Supreme Court, which ruled that Santeria followers had a right to their rites.

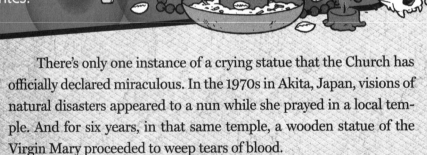

WHAT'S HAPPENING, DUDES?

There's only one instance of a crying statue that the Church has officially declared miraculous. In the 1970s in Akita, Japan, visions of natural disasters appeared to a nun while she prayed in a local temple. And for six years, in that same temple, a wooden statue of the Virgin Mary proceeded to weep tears of blood.

There are two schools of thought on the weeping Akita statue. Catholic authorities say: It's a miracle! They investigated the matter and declared the visions and tears a supernatural occurrence. But there are also plenty of skeptics who say the weeping statue was simply a hoax that went undetected.

SHARP MEMORIES

One. Two.

Hold still. It will only hurt for a minute...

Three.

Three small slices with a razor blade, until blood runs freely down the forehead.

That's how some fathers in Lebanon mark their children, teaching them about the martyrdom of Imam Hussein.

In 680 CE, Hussein took a small group of men and battled against a huge army, fighting for better, more strictly Islamic, rule. His force was brutally defeated. Hussein and his men were beheaded, and their bodies left on the battlefield to rot in the sun.

Today, the Shiite Muslim faith honors the anniversary of Hussein's death. Some followers bring their offspring to the ritual, where their foreheads are cut three times. The children's blood flows just as Hussein's blood flowed. Other Shiite believers join annual marches, where some of the men cut themselves with razors or knives.

TOP FIVE REASONS FOR A BLOODY SACRIFICE

1. The dead need slaves. And wives. Maybe some pets. Bury a few live folks with a dead king or pharaoh, and our ruler will have plenty of help in the afterlife.

2. The classic suck-up. If we give the gods our best, maybe they'll repay the favor.

3. That whole cycle-of-life thing. We give to the gods, the gods give to the earth, the earth gives to us. Please pass the corn.

4. The ultimate apology. Our bad. Take this lamb as a symbol of our regret.

5. Immortality. Now that we've given this blood, we'd like to live forever and ever . . . deal?

Clerics have spoken out against this tradition of drawing blood, saying that it breaks the Islamic rule against harming one's body. But each year, people continue to show their faith with blood offerings.

Once you look closely, almost every religion on earth seems to have some rules and rituals related to blood. After all, religions are about explaining life—and our ancestors could see the link between life and the blood pulsing in our veins.

Harker's Personal Notes

My unanswered questions:

💀 You'd think a civilization would be . . . well, civilized. The Aztecs had amazing gardens and complicated legal systems, but they also tore the hearts out of live victims!

💀 Do humans have some sort of built-in bloodlust? Why else would so many societies make offerings of blood?

💀 Is it okay to sacrifice animals for religious reasons? How is that different than killing for meat, or hunting for sport?

CHAPTER 2
RITES OF PASSAGE

YOU WANT TO BE AN ADULT? Can you handle the responsibility?

You might not be so eager if you lived in the mountains of Papua New Guinea.

Every year, teen and young adult Matausa men follow their elders into the jungle for a bloody initiation ritual. The Matausa believe that in order to become fully recognized adults, able to marry and have children, young men must first cleanse themselves of their mothers' blood. After all, those moms! They hug you, they kiss you, they stick food in your mouth. Seriously. It's time to wash all that mommy business away.

BUT I WANT MY MOMMY!

The ceremony includes a number of gruesome challenges intended to cleanse a young man's insides of any lingering maternal blood and eliminate the influence of his mother's milk. At one point, an elder slices the inside of the initiate's nose until it bleeds.

At the end of the ritual, the child who suckled milk from his mother, or had his scrapes kissed and coddled, no longer exists. Now, there's a man in his place—a full-grown, self-sufficient, mommy-free man.

LIMITED TIME OFFER

Attract more women!
Feel stronger!
Gain energy!
Prove your bravery!

Does this sound like the latest infomercial, or a spam e-mail for a vitamin cocktail? Maybe. But attractiveness, strength, energy, courage—these are all appealing attributes that many people want. And they're exactly the results that young people seek when they endure an initiation ceremony like the one practiced by the Matausa people.

All over the world, different kinds of blood rites mark the time when boys come of age and become full members of their societies. The rites symbolize the transformation from child to mature, responsible adult.

In another part of Papua New Guinea, along the Sepik River, people believe that the first humans were created by mythological crocodiles. Initiates entering manhood in this region endure tiny slices across their chests, backs, and buttocks. The young men are accompanied by their uncles to a spirit house away from the main village, where men known as "cutters," specially trained by the elders, make hundreds of incisions on their bodies. Each cut represents the mark of a crocodile's tooth. The initiates' skin, permanently scarred by the ceremony, eventually heals and is said to resemble the bumpy, scaly skin of a crocodile.

SKIN DEEP

In Ethiopia, girls in the Karo tribe have tiny cuts made on their bellies, beginning when they're about five years old. The cuts continue until the girls are ready to marry, by which time the patterns of scars have made them beautiful in the eyes of their people. Karo men also scar themselves, to represent their ferocity. For them, each scar symbolizes a slain enemy.

MALE BONDING, EXTREME VERSION

In the past, there were many traditional initiation ceremonies for young men. And they shared similarities, even though they were performed in vastly different parts of the world. They involved pain. They involved blood. They involved facing and overcoming fear, and pledging a deep allegiance to the group. After all, many of these men would be physically, permanently marked as members of their societies. That was serious commitment!

Some of these rites are still practiced today, either traditionally or with a modern approach:

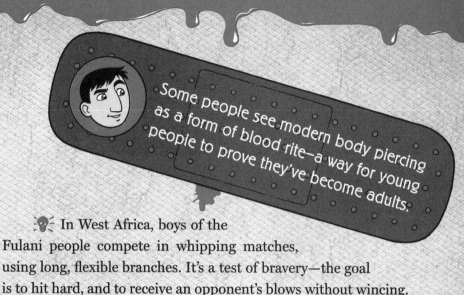

Some people see modern body piercing as a form of blood rite—a way for young people to prove they've become adults.

In West Africa, boys of the Fulani people compete in whipping matches, using long, flexible branches. It's a test of bravery—the goal is to hit hard, and to receive an opponent's blows without wincing.

In parts of Polynesia, tattoos marked family ties and were first done when boys reached adolescence. Sharpened needles were dipped in ashes and then pounded into the skin—a slow, bloody, and excruciating process. Some say the word "tattoo," or *tatau*, comes from the tapping sound of hammer on needle. Missionaries tried to stop tattooing in the 1800s and early 1900s, and there are now more modern methods available. Still, some young men choose to undergo the traditional procedures.

Maasai men on the African savanna traditionally proved their adulthood through lion hunting—

BLOOD WINGS

When American soldiers graduate from military flight school, they receive their parachutist badges, also known as jump wings. The instructor pins a badge to each soldier's uniform—but doesn't tuck the pin into the latch. Instead, the pin is left open, pointing directly toward the soldier's skin. Then the instructor or a friend launches himself at the graduate, driving the pin directly into the soldier's chest.

This is a sort of initiation ceremony called "blood wings." It's officially banned by the U.S. Armed Forces, it's highly controversial . . . and it's a badge of honor for those who ignore the rules and endure it. A modern blood rite.

sometimes even going solo. Killing a lion involves finding the creature, taunting it into a rage, and slaying it using only a spear and shield. Lion hunting still occurs among the Maasai, but to protect the lion populations, they now hunt less often, and mainly in groups.

An anthropologist at the University of Connecticut spent years traveling the world to study male initiation rituals of the past and present. He found that in groups where pain and blood are involved in coming-of-age rites, there's usually one strong commonality: war. These are societies where battle can be fierce and frequent. By committing to the group and by facing pain and blood, young men are showing they can be courageous. They can be ferocious. They can be warriors!

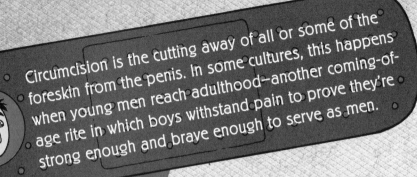

Circumcision is the cutting away of all or some of the foreskin from the penis. In some cultures, this happens when young men reach adulthood—another coming-of-age rite in which boys withstand pain to prove they're strong enough and brave enough to serve as men.

GIRL POWER

For girls, there's no need to create a bloody ritual when childhood ends and adulthood begins. It happens all on its own!

When puberty hits, girls experience their first menstrual period. Each month, a young woman's ovaries will release an egg, and the egg will travel to the uterus. If the egg isn't fertilized (in other words, the woman isn't pregnant), the uterus releases its lining, causing four or five days of bleeding.

In almost every culture, a girl's first menstrual period is considered a sign of

DARN, I JUST GOT MY PERIOD.

LA-LA-LA! I CAN'T HEAR YOU!

change, fertility, and womanhood. There are big differences in the ways girls are treated, though, when they officially become women.

In some traditional societies, girls are showered with gifts and pampered like queens. Among the Asante people of Ghana, a girl who gets her first period is seated under a large umbrella—a sun-shade usually reserved for royalty. She's presented with elaborate gifts, and dancers and singers perform in her honor. In Zambia, girls are fed ceremonial foods, bathed in medicine, and involved in a ceremonial dance for fertility. And in what is now the southern United States, ancient Pueblo rituals involved treating a girl as a goddess—the Earth Mother—for four days.

Unfortunately for girls, other ways of marking this passage into adulthood are not so celebratory. In some Muslim societies, like the rural farming villages of Turkey, people believe that men-struation occurs because the first woman disobeyed God and brought impurity into the world. In other cultures, people believe that menstrual blood is polluting, or dirty. On the farms in south-ern Portugal, for example, local lore says that a woman with her period can't help prepare pork or make sausages—if she does, the meat will spoil. Among the Beng people of the Ivory Coast, a menstruating woman can't work in the fields, or the crops will fail. She is sent to spend a week in a separate hut, isolated from the men of her village.

That tradition of seclusion—creating a separate place for menstruating girls and women to stay—was once common in many places, from the Pacific coast of North America to central Africa. It's still practiced by traditional societ-ies in places such as India, Sierra Leone, and Indonesia.

PRIVATE CLUBHOUSE. KEEP OUT!

In societies where menstruating girls and women are isolated, there's usually the same basic explanation. Menstrual blood is dirty. Isolating the girls protects the guys, not to mention the whole village. Who knows what spoiled meat and disease and other havoc those women might create?

For years, anthropologists have studied these customs. Until recently, they've believed that when women are isolated, it means men hold all the power. The women are being punished, in a way. After all, no one would *want* to be sent into seclusion. Right?

Right?

Hmmm...

In recent decades, anthropologists have suggested a new way of looking at things. It turns out that life as a woman in a traditional rural village isn't all that easy. You have to tend the fields, and sometimes the animals. You have to carry the water from the river or the well. You have to cook for your family, and wash the clothes, and watch the children, and scrub the pots, and weave the baskets, and tend the fire, and...

Whew! Maybe that time in the menstrual hut is a vacation!

At the very least, it's probably a time when women can bond with one another, without the overwhelming workload. They can tell traditional stories, pass on knowledge of healing and child-birth, and teach girls what it means to be women.

POISON AND POWER

Whether or not seclusion is a symbol of male dominance, there's no question that men-strual blood makes many men—and even women—uncomfortable. Maybe that's how it gained its reputation as a potent ingredient in potions. Menstrual blood has been used in love spells in medieval France, parts of Africa, and the southern United States.

Or, let's say you have your eye on someone new. Someone pretty. But you already have a girlfriend. If you're a Mae Enga man from Papua New Guinea, look out! If you flirt with the new girl, your girlfriend might use her menstrual blood to poison you. In that culture, it's a well-known way to get revenge.

Menstrual blood was also used as poison by the priests of the Asante people in Ghana, who placed it on small ornaments,

The aboriginal people of Australia prized ochre as a pigment for art and for body paint during dances and rituals. The deep red color of the mineral often represented blood, believed to bring strength, healing, and protection.

or "fetishes,"
with sacred meaning. It
wasn't likely to actually harm anyone, but
the power of belief is a potent thing! By carrying these symbols, the priests felt they would be protected from evil. Women of the Kwakiutl people on the northwest coast of North America believed in menstrual blood's poisonous powers, too. They kept some stored on shredded bark, as protection against monsters.

But just as sacrificial blood in religious rites is used both as a symbol of life and a symbol of death, menstrual blood can represent pollution and poison, or it can bring new

MENSTRUAL MEDICINE?

The ancient Roman philosopher Pliny the Elder wrote that menstrual blood could be made into a poultice and used to treat all sorts of ailments, from gout to worms, and from hemorrhages to headaches. (He also said it could be held up to the sky during lightning storms to prevent hail.)

In the early 1900s, a French doctor used injections of menstrual blood to treat liver disease. According to him, the treatments were quite successful.

life and fertility. The connection between menstruation and child-bearing wasn't lost on early societies, though they didn't interpret the connection in quite the same way we do today.

For example, if you were one of the Tiv people in what is now Nigeria, you might have wanted good crops for the next year, and lots of babies born in the village. Here's what you'd have needed for the *imborivungu*, or "owl pipe," fertility ritual:

- Blood from a sacrificed child
- Menstrual blood
- A bowl for mixing it
- A pipe for smoking it

If that didn't make the crops grow, what would?

A driver's license, a high school diploma, a first paycheck: these are some of the ways we now mark adulthood. They're non-physical symbols, with no painful rituals required. But in the past, in many parts of the world, maturity was measured in blood.

Harker's Personal Notes

I need time to THINK! My latest questions . . .

💀 Why does the shedding of blood mark the end of childhood? I don't have to cut myself to prove I'm mature . . . do I?

💀 Do we still have coming-of-age ceremonies? How do my friends prove that they're not kids anymore?

💀 Why would women WANT to shut themselves in a hut?

CHAPTER 3
SIPS AND SUPPERS

FRY A GENEROUS HELPING of onions in butter and lard. Stir in cream, spices, and salt and pepper. Add blood, mixing carefully to prevent lumps. Using a funnel, fill prepared sausage casings. Cook for about half an hour in simmering water. When casing is pricked with a sharp knife, juices should run clear.

Sound tasty? That's a recipe for blood sausage, similar to what the British call black pudding. People eat variations of the dish in Europe, South America, North America, and parts of Asia. In the Basque region of Spain, it's made with diced leeks; in Tuscany, cooks add pine nuts and raisins to create *sanguinaccio*.

Though some of us blanch at the idea, blood is an important ingredient in all sorts of traditional foods. Here are a few more red and relished dishes from around the world:

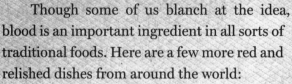 Yak blood cubes: Tibetan herders draw a small portion of blood from a living yak, then simmer the liquid in a shallow pan until it congeals and can be sliced into cubes.

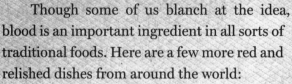 Chinese "blood tofu": Also served in congealed cubes, this is made with duck or pig blood and skewered on a stick, like a shish kebab.

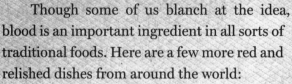 Cow's blood: The Maasai of Africa drink milk mixed with cow's blood to celebrate special occasions, or to speed healing.

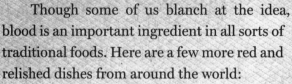 Seal's blood: In Canada's Arctic, Inuit people drink this raw, believing it brings strength to their own circulatory systems.

In some of the places where humans have incorporated blood into their diets, it's partly because protein is scarce. Seal's blood probably does bring strength to the Inuit, since it's naturally high in protein and iron.

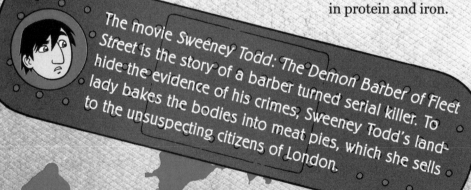

The movie Sweeney Todd: The Demon Barber of Fleet Street is the story of a barber turned serial killer. To hide the evidence of his crimes, Sweeney Todd's landlady bakes the bodies into meat pies, which she sells to the unsuspecting citizens of London.

In the depths of the Arctic winter or high on the Tibetan plateaus, any source of nourishment is valuable.

In other cultures, dishes made with blood allow people to use an entire animal, and prevent waste. There are technical reasons, too, for cooking with blood. For example, it acts as a thickener. Ancient Mongolian cooks knew this when they used blood in their noodle recipes and the Mesopotamians understood it when they served turnips slathered in blood sauce. Today, modern Filipino cooks see the same thing when they watch a bowl of *dinuguan*—blood stew—thicken on the stove.

BLOOD AND GUTS

AH... RARE, BLOODY, AND DELICIOUS.

So why do we like steak dripping with blood-red juice, but refuse to try gelatinous blood cubes? Why do we wrinkle our noses when blood soup is offered? And why aren't we all taste-testing *tiet canh*, a Vietnamese dish made with duck blood?

It's possible that eating blood reminds us too vividly that we're feasting on what was once a living creature.

Blodplättar for breakfast? They may not appear on the IKEA lunch menu, but blood pancakes, or blodplättar, are traditional Swedish fare. They're made just like regular pancakes, but with half milk and half blood, plus a dash of marjoram for flavor.

(But then, how do we explain people's love of rare steak?) Or perhaps the flavor is too similar to that of our own blood. We all know what it tastes like when we bite our tongue too hard. Who wants to savor *that* for supper? Some anthropologists have suggested that we fear eating blood because humans have evolved as predators. We hunt, we kill, and we eat. Feasting on blood could trigger a shark-like feeding frenzy and we wouldn't be able to stop! Okay, maybe that's a bit extreme, but a taste for blood *is* something we would have in common with predators of the animal kingdom, such as lions and grizzlies.

And yet . . . if these theories were true, they would apply to *all* people. Instead, the aversion to eating blood seems to be a cultural issue. Lots of people in northern Britain love black pudding. But many in southern Britain hate it. Diners in the Canadian province of Quebec eat blood sausage, and people a few hours away in the province of Ontario won't touch the stuff.

Basically, it comes down to the way we're trained to think. Just as ways of viewing menstrual blood vary from culture to culture, so do feelings about eating animal blood. If we grow up where curry with blood sauce is a family specialty, we'll dig in! If we're raised where our neighbors and parents think eating blood is distasteful . . . we probably won't be craving black pudding any time soon.

THOU SHALT NOT

deas about eating or not eating blood aren't just randomly passed through families. In some cases, they're a matter of religion.

For example, many Jewish people adhere to a Hebrew Bible passage which reads, "The life of every creature is its blood. That is why I have said to the Israelites, 'You must not eat the blood of any creature, because the life of every creature is its blood; anyone who eats it must be cut off.'"

No one wants to be cut off at dinnertime! That's why, for some Jewish families, meat is drained and salted to remove the blood and make it "kosher," okay to eat.

Islamic beliefs are somewhat similar, and there are specific rules for making meat "halal," or allowed. The Islamic holy book, the Qur'an, reads, "Forbidden to you are carrion, blood, and flesh of swine." As in the Jewish tradition, meat is drained of blood before it is eaten.

IS THIS STUFF KOSHER?

SNIFF SNIFF

HEAD VS. HEARTBEAT

"Put that brain of yours to work!"

"Use your head!"

"Put your thinking caps on!"

Teachers everywhere use those lines. Two thousand years ago, they would have chosen different catchphrases. They might have said, "Put that blood of yours to work," or "Use your heart!"

The people of ancient Rome and early Europe believed the heart was the center of the body—sort of the way astronomers once thought the earth was the center of the universe. They believed emotion and intellect pumped out of our hearts and flowed through our flesh along with our blood. All those neurons that we now know fire through the brain to keep us conscious? Doctors thought those functions were served by the circulatory system.

I PRICKED MY FINGER! NOW MY SMARTS ARE LEAKING OUT!

Is it any wonder that people came up with rules for eating blood? It represented life force, consciousness, even a creature's soul.

We can't know for sure if this is why certain religions banned the consumption of blood. It may also have been because blood was a highly symbolic fluid, used in rituals and traditional sacrifices. Excluding it from the daily diet made it something more special, and more divine. Or perhaps in the days before refrigeration and health inspectors, draining and salting meat made it safer to eat.

For true believers, of course, none of these explanations matters. They only need one reason to avoid blood: the word of God.

THE EXTRA-WILD KINGDOM

Animals have no qualms about eating the red stuff. Here are a few of the world's most bloodthirsty species:

☠ In Mexico and South America, vampire bats feed on both mammals and birds. After using their teeth to nick a creature's skin, they lick up the ooze.

☠ Once attached to a mammal's skin, a leech will suck so much blood that its body will swell to several times its original size. It can live for months on one meal.

☠ With a long, nose-like tube called a proboscis, a female mosquito can pierce a mammal's skin and drink the blood she needs for her body to create eggs.

☠ Some species of lamprey, an eel-like fish, feed on the blood of other fish.

☠ Found in Asia and southern Europe, vampire moths slurp animal blood with a proboscis similar to that of a mosquito.

THE GRAIL

Care for a nice cuppa blood? If *eating* blood has prompted all sorts of stories, traditions, and cultural rules, *drinking* blood has spawned even more. In Europe, some of the most interesting tales relate to a sacred object known as the Holy Grail.

Historically speaking, legends of the Holy Grail are a big, fat mess. The grail itself is said to be the cup used by Jesus at the Last Supper, before he was crucified. Jesus took the cup and called the wine it held a symbol of his blood.

To that, we add the story of Joseph, the man who apparently provided a tomb for Jesus. Somewhere along the way to the burial site, he caught a few drops of Jesus' blood in the grail. Then, he sent the grail to Britain to be protected.

I'LL BE YOUNG AGAIN IN A JIFFY!

Next, we mix in some stories from ancient Britain—tales of King Arthur, Knights of the Round Table, and a brave and determined Welsh lad named Percival. The result: a series of semi-religious legends about a miraculous cup, said to hold the power of immortality. Anyone who drank from the grail would be fully healed of whatever ailed him or her, and would understand—in an instant—the full power of God.

There are countless variations of the legend of the Holy Grail, and just as many noble quests to find it. In all of them, the grail has a connection to great healing power. Because it touched the blood of Jesus, the cup absorbed some of God's ability to perform miracles.

It's a prime example of the law of contagion.

1. Item A is extra-cool.

2. Item B touches Item A.

3. Item B gets a hint of cool.

Does that sound impossible? Illogical? Think of it this way: a movie star kisses your hand. Your skin tingles, and you vow never to wash your hand again.

Or, you meet someone who has an incurable disease, such as AIDS. AIDS is a disease that affects the immune system, and it can only be caught if you share bodily fluids—blood, for example—with someone who already has AIDS. You can't catch it through casual contact.

You understand all of this, but then your new acquaintance gives you his scarf. There's no way that the scarf touched any blood . . . but do you immediately wrap it around your neck?

According to experiments by modern psychologists, you'll probably choose not to wear the scarf. Oh, you know you're being unreasonable. You know that the scarf is perfectly safe. But somewhere deep down inside, you feel like it's contaminated. Why? The law of contagion—which isn't really a law at all, just a superstition.

When it comes to blood, people have come up with all sorts of law-of-contagion strategies. In Renaissance Europe, women used moisturizer made from the blood of white doves, hoping the birds' purity and pallor would transfer to human skin. In the Middle Ages, the blood of execution victims was believed to hold energy. After all, these people hadn't died of disease; they had been killed in the prime of life. Onlookers dipped pieces of cloth in the victims' blood to create energy-filled souvenirs.

In one of the goriest examples of contagion, Roman gladiators drank the blood of their opponents.

Yes, you read that correctly. They raged through the Coliseum, slaughtering other gladiators for the entertainment of thousands of cheering fans. Then they drank their blood, believing that the strength and bravery of the dead fighters would transfer into their own bodies.

In ancient Egypt, pharaohs bathed in blood to protect themselves from leprosy, a contagious disease causing skin sores, nerve damage, and breathing problems.

On special occasions, the fans were allowed to drink blood, too.

This kind of thinking isn't restricted to the ancient past. When Mother Teresa died in 1997 after dedicating her life to serving India's poor, she was beatified by the Catholic pope—a step on the way to sainthood. Drops of her blood were collected to display as relics, items from a saint's body that are sometimes believed to have miraculous powers of healing.

Some of the people who believe in these relics are highly educated, urban, modern citizens—a far cry from the mob in the Roman Coliseum. Yet they subscribe to the power of blood, and a form of the law of contagion.

FOUL FANGS

Eating blood. Drinking blood. Connecting blood with vigor and strength. Eventually, these ideas all lead to one creature: the vampire.

From the Dark Ages of Transylvania to the *Twilight*-obsessed readers of the 21st century, vampire myths have held lasting power. Variations of the blood-sucking monster exist in Russia,

Africa, India, Brazil, and Mexico. In Albania, a vampire can be killed with a knife through the heart. In Crete, the creature should be beheaded, and the head boiled in vinegar.

According to the legends of some regions, people become vampires as a sort of cosmic punishment for terrible crimes. More commonly, though, the world's vampires seem to arise from three possible scenarios:

1. An improper burial,
2. A violent death, or
3. A tragic love affair.

At its most basic, the vampire myth is yet another connection between blood and life force. If you lose enough blood, you die. So maybe if you're dead, and you manage to drink blood, you'll gain a new life . . . sort of. Plus, if a restless spirit is going to haunt the earth, it's going to need sustenance . . . and what better food than soul-carrying, emotion-feeding, life-giving blood?

In one Japanese legend, an evil vampire cat sucks the blood from the most beautiful woman in the prince's palace. It then transforms into a demon version of the woman and takes her place at the prince's side. Meow.

In Spanish tales, executioners regularly dine on meat pastries made with the blood of their victims.

REAL-LIFE VAMP

In the early 1600s, a Hungarian countess named Elizabeth Bathory was known for her interest in the occult. According to local lore, she once beat a young servant so badly that the poor girl's blood splashed onto the countess's skin. Later, she grew convinced that the area of skin where the blood had touched looked younger than the skin on the rest of her body.

Countess Bathory began bathing regularly in blood—a habit that led to the disappearance of so many young girls that the king of Hungary sent investigators. Eventually convicted of 80 murders, the countess was imprisoned in her castle for the remainder of her life.

This isn't the only blood-soaked tale to come from eastern Europe. Because vampire tales were part of the region's mythology, a plague or a series of sudden deaths could sometimes set the stage for vampire mania. In the 1700s, Empress Maria Theresa of Austria heard stories about people mutilating bodies to ensure they didn't spring back to life as vampires. The empress sent her doctor to investigate, and he uncovered a tangled web of superstition, twisted religious beliefs, and rumor. One executioner had claimed that blood gushed from a corpse—a sure indicator of a vampire

MODERN SLAYERS

💀 Between 1997 and 2003, viewers tuned in weekly to watch *Buffy the Vampire Slayer* battle the forces of darkness. The idea that a petite teenage girl could rid the world of vampires gained the show millions of loyal fans.

💀 In the 2004 action film *Van Helsing*, actor Hugh Jackman is sent by an order of Vatican-based knights to defeat not only a series of vampires, but a werewolf and Frankenstein's monster as well.

💀 The Vampire Chronicles by Anne Rice spanned 11 books, which sold a total of 80 million copies. The 1994 film *Interview with the Vampire* was based on the first book in the series, and made the vampire character Lestat famous around the world.

about to rise. Later, he admitted that only a small trickle of blood had run from the body.

In the 1700s and 1800s, trade and travel were increasing between eastern Europe and countries to the west. Along with these new exchanges went the vampire stories of eastern European mythology. Writers—particularly those in Britain—seized on these tales for inspiration, and vampires made their way into a host of gothic poems and novels. Today, the most famous of these is Bram Stoker's *Dracula*, published in 1897. A young lawyer imprisoned in a shadowy castle, three attractive but dangerous vampire women, and the evil Count Dracula himself—what reader could ask for more?

I WANT TO SUCK YOUR BLOOD!

...FOR MEDICINAL REASONS, OF COURSE!

Historians have suggested that there were actual blood drinkers in Transylvania. These people may have suffered from porphyria (por-FEE-ree-a), a genetic blood disorder that causes nervous-system disorders and skin problems, including extreme sensitivity to sunlight. Theoretically, a pale and sickly porphyria sufferer could have gained strength from drinking iron-rich blood. Possible? Perhaps. But most historians believe the connection is unlikely.

BOTTLED UP

In the years following World War II, new technology allowed doctors to give donated blood—and a boost of strength—to someone who was injured or sick. These blood transfusions grew more common around the world. Procedures weren't always safe, though, and not only because the technology was experimental. In one instance, a group of Tanganyikan people in Africa's Ivory Coast attacked a Red Cross medical camp. Apparently, they had seen blood samples near bottles of wine and thought that the Red Cross employees were drinking Tanganyikan blood.

FATAL ATTRACTION

Why did Victorian readers find tales of blood-sucking monsters so enthralling? And why do vampires continue to top the bestseller lists today?

It could be the delicious shiver of fear—the lurking danger of death—that leads people to vampire tales. Then, of course, there's the eternal question: If you could trade death for everlasting life, even if immortality came with its own curses ... would you? Would you make the trade?

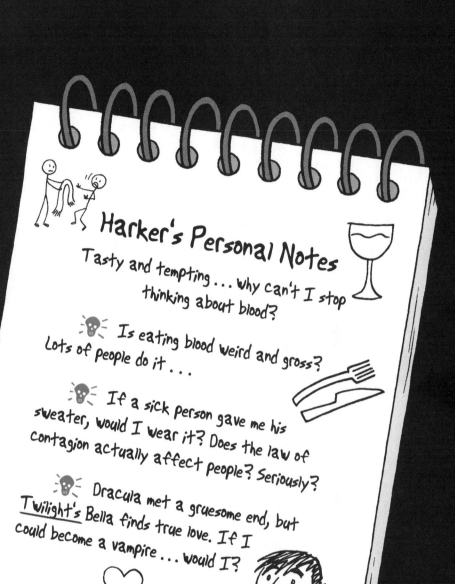

Harker's Personal Notes

Tasty and tempting... why can't I stop thinking about blood?

Is eating blood weird and gross? Lots of people do it...

If a sick person gave me his sweater, would I wear it? Does the law of contagion actually affect people? Seriously?

Dracula met a gruesome end, but _Twilight's_ Bella finds true love. If I could become a vampire... would I?

CHAPTER 4
TIES THAT BIND

LIKE FATHER, LIKE SON. Like mother, like daughter. Ancient people didn't need degrees in genetics to recognize that physical characteristics and personality traits ran through families. They believed that blood was passed from parent to child, and members of the same extended family shared the same blood.

In many parts of the world, sharing the blood of an extended family provided safety. Your elders would ensure you had enough to eat. Your brothers would fight to protect your land. Your aunts and uncles would prepare you for work, or marriage, or war. If you had a disagreement with someone, the head of your family could serve as a judge.

In Scotland, this sort of large family group was called a clan, and the clans ruled the land from the fifth to the eighteenth century. If you were born during that time, you knew your family not only by shared blood, but also by shared tartans, symbols, ceremonies, and songs. Some Scottish clans even became known for specific skills. The members of one clan might be healers, and the members of another would be skilled musicians. For the people of the Highlands, being part of a group of blood relatives offered safety in numbers, a sense of belonging, and all the resources that many able bodies could provide.

But dividing the world into fiercely loyal family groups isn't always the best way to keep the peace. North of Greece, in the mountains of Montenegro, clans of the 1700s and 1800s struggled to survive on rugged slopes with poor cropland. They constantly fought with other clans. The murder of someone in one family would lead to murder or revenge in another. Back and forth it would go in an endless blood feud—the blood of one family taken in payment for the blood of another.

Modern historians have suggested that the people of the region would have been better off if they had stopped fighting and focused on trade instead—or if the clans had worked together for the common good. But for the people of Montenegro, spilling blood seemed the only answer.

CALF'S BLOOD: THE WONDER DRUG!

Remember Claudius Galen, the second-century Roman doctor and philosopher who discovered that blood flowed through the body? He believed that because blood traveled through the liver, the heart, and the brain, it gathered the characteristics of those organs. Basically, he thought blood carried personality.

BLOOD RUNS DEEP

The connection between blood and personality still exists today—at least in language. Have you ever heard these phrases?

- 💀 He's hot-blooded.
- 💀 Her blood ran cold.
- 💀 That makes my blood boil!
- 💀 I was so angry, I could taste blood.

Apparently, modern medicine hasn't completely erased our old beliefs.

Let's jump ahead to the 1600s. Hundreds of years after Galen came up with his theory, people *still* believed blood carried character traits. They also believed—correctly—that blood traveled through arteries and veins on its circuit of the body. They knew that if they cut a blood vessel in a dog and sewed one end of it to a blood vessel in a second dog, blood would flow from one animal into the other.

These doctors attempted some of the first blood transfusions—transferring blood from a strong animal to a sick person in the hope that new strength would flow with the new blood. Talk about experimental treatment! Usually, the procedure proved fatal. The doctors didn't quite know what they were doing, and they were basing their techniques on a strange mix of fresh ideas and old superstitions.

For example, they still believed in Galen's theory that blood carried character traits. And if people could exchange blood . . . well, a blood transfusion might change a person's personality.

In 1667, a doctor named Jean-Baptiste Denis took a mentally ill and violent man off the streets and transfused him with calf's blood, hoping the calf's calm nature would soothe the man.

Jean-Baptiste was no quack. He was one of the French king's personal physicians and a highly respected man. Plus, the transfusion worked. Well, okay…the man developed a fever, peed blood, and writhed in pain. But he survived! He also stayed calm for several weeks afterwards, and the process was declared a medical miracle.

Today, we know that the poor man was suffering from intense shock, and was lucky to live through the procedure. Several similar experiments by other doctors ended in death. And after that, blood transfusions were temporarily banned in Europe.

They didn't become commonplace until the early 1900s. By that time, doctors knew more about blood and worried less about personality types—the procedures were purely scientific. But did they manage to entirely separate emotions from transfusions? Not quite.

If you receive a transfusion today, the blood will come from a blood bank—an organization that collects and stores donations. You'll never know who, exactly, provided the blood used for your

transfusion. Blood banks keep that information secret on purpose. They don't want blood recipients to feel as if they *owe* the donors, and they don't want donors and recipients to feel connected. After all, transfusions are about saving lives, not about creating blood ties, or new family relationships.

ROYAL BLOOD

Prince William is destined for the English throne. He'll take tea at Buckingham Palace and tour the Commonwealth to be feted and honored. He'll be treated like ... well, like royalty! Why? Because he was born of royal blood.

In most monarchies, the right to rule is passed from father to eldest son. If that eldest son has warts on his nose, or a terrible disease, or isn't very bright—it doesn't matter. He was born to rule; it's in his blood.

Today, England is a democracy and people vote for their leaders. Old ideas about royals having the right to rule no longer apply. But many of the world's kings and queens still exist, at least as figureheads. We treat them like superstars. And even if they

The Morganatic Boy: half king, half commoner

have less power now, their very existence proves that we continue to believe in bloodlines.

In countries such as Jordan, Morocco, Thailand, Britain, Bhutan, Norway, and Japan, crowns and scepters are passed from generation to generation. All because people accept that royal blood makes a certain family better, more impressive, and more downright regal.

Rules about the purity of royal blood have grown less strict in most countries. Prince William raised eyebrows in 2011 by being the first British royal to marry—gasp!—a commoner. Hundreds of years ago, however, royals only married royals. If you were in line to inherit the crown, your chances depended on exactly how much royal blood ran through your veins. If only one of your parents was royal, then you had morganatic blood—half-blood, in other words—and you had no claim to the throne.

To give their children, and their children's children, the best chance at staying in power (and to make friends with neighboring countries) kings and queens arranged marriages between their kids and those of other royal families. In Europe, princes from England married princesses from France, and princesses from Spain married princes from Austria. Eventually, the royal families of Europe were tied together in a tangle of bloodlines that only the most dedicated historian could unravel.

At one point, there were hundreds of monarchies around the world. Today, there are still 44, although the king or queen has absolute power in only six.

THE QUEEN'S GENES

Check out this tiny branch of a royal family tree: in the 1800s, England's Queen Victoria had five daughters and four sons, who married various royals all over Europe. One married the emperor of Germany, and one married a grand duchess of Russia. Queen Victoria had 42 grandchildren, too, and more than half of them married into royal families.

There was just one problem with all this royal knot-tying: genetic disease.

Hundreds of years ago, people had no idea that along with a birthright to the throne, royal bloodlines could carry defective genes. Genes that caused diseases such as porphyria and hemophilia. Genes that would wreak havoc all over Europe.

Porphyria—the same sensitivity to sunlight that may have sparked vampire myths in eastern Europe—could have caused King George III's mental illness in the early 1800s and sent him to his seclusion in Windsor Castle. Historians believe other royals, including four of George's children, may have suffered from this condition as well.

A few decades later, Queen Victoria introduced an even more destructive strain of blood into Europe's royal families. She carried the gene for hemophilia, a disease that is passed on by women, but which usually only affects men. When a hemophiliac is cut or bruised, his blood doesn't clot properly, and his body has trouble stopping the bleeding. A small cut becomes a major ordeal, and a fall or head injury can be fatal.

Victoria's wayward gene would eventually affect her son Leopold, and her grandsons Frederick, Leopold, and Maurice. One of Victoria's granddaughters became queen of Spain and one became tsarina of Russia—both carried the gene for hemophilia.

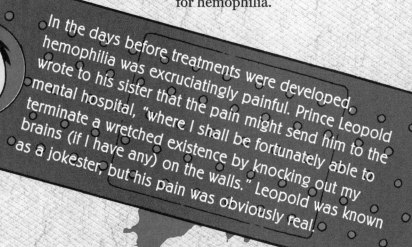

In the days before treatments were developed, hemophilia was excruciatingly painful. Prince Leopold wrote to his sister that the pain might send him to the mental hospital, "where I shall be fortunately able to terminate a wretched existence by knocking out my brains (if I have any) on the walls." Leopold was known as a jokester, but his pain was obviously real.

THE BLEEDERS

HMMM...

People have known about hemophilia since ancient times. The Talmud, a Jewish holy book, instructed that if two baby brothers had died after circumcision, other males in that family didn't have to be circumcised at birth. And Arab histories tell of a family of brothers who died from bleeding.

In 1803, a researcher tracked hemophiliacs through a number of families. Doctors were convinced that "the bleeding disease" ran through bloodlines. They still didn't know what caused it. Some suggested that sufferers had weak blood vessels, easily broken. One outspoken doctor called it the male version of menstruation. Finally, in 1891, a scientist named Almroth Wright took various blood samples and proved that when put into test tubes, the blood of hemophiliacs took much longer to thicken and clot.

Eventually, researchers discovered the exact ingredients in blood that would help it clot, and they found ways to inject patients' veins with these "clotting factors." Modern hemophiliacs can travel with their own medical supplies, and live relatively normal lives. But the royal hemophiliacs of Europe weren't so lucky—these discoveries were all still generations away.

THE ROYAL DISEASE

Queen Victoria's blood traveled all over Europe. Some historians say it even changed the course of history. They say if wild Prince Edward had inherited hemophilia as Leopold did, one of his more stable brothers would have worn the crown.

They theorize that a series of ill or hemophiliac heirs to the Spanish throne destabilized the country and helped lead to the Spanish Civil War. Others wonder whether the tsar of Russia and his wife were too focused on the health of their hemophiliac son to care for the country. While they were busy worrying, the Russian Revolution began, which eventually led to the birth of the Soviet Union.

Was it all because of a blood-borne disease?

BLUE BLOODS

If you visited a Spanish market in the 1800s, you'd see a melting pot of people and cultures. There were Christians and Jews, darker-skinned Moorish people descended from past invaders, fair folks visiting from the north, and every variation of skin color in between. In the mansions of Castile, however, lived members of an aristocracy who would never mix with such rabble. These nobles prided themselves on their pure, untainted, and extremely white genetic stock. Their skin was so pale, they could see the blue veins on the insides of their wrists. These Spanish snobs were the *sangre azul*, the original blue bloods.

When the phrase passed into English usage, "blue blood" came to mean anyone from an aristocratic family. And in North America, it can mean anyone from a rich and established family—although probably still a *white*, rich, and established family.

BLOOD BONDS

Queen Victoria knew something was wrong with her blood-line, but she married her kids into royal families all over Europe. She did everything possible to make her children successful, no matter what the cost to other people.

It all goes to show: blood is thicker than water.

That's a phrase we use to explain our family ties. Given a choice between protecting our family and protecting our friends, we'll choose our family. Our blood ties keep us loyal, devoted, and true. They keep us tightly bound to one another. The connections between us and our unrelated friends, on the other hand, are as weak and insubstantial as water.

But what if we could strengthen our ties with outsiders? What if we could feel as connected, and as loyal, to outsiders as to our own family? In some cases, people have used blood, and the exchange of blood, as the symbol for this kind of connection.

The idea of a blood brotherhood has existed for centuries, and many believe it originated in the rites of different African peoples. The phrase

Today, because we know that diseases such as AIDS and hepatitis C can be passed through blood, we're extra careful about touching other people's bodily fluids. But kids weren't always so careful. You might try asking your grandpa—did he ever have a blood brother?

appeared in English literature for the first time in a book called *The Founding of the Congo Free State* by Henry Morton Stanley, written in 1885. Describing his encounter with a new group of locals, Stanley wrote: "The next day we made blood brotherhood. The fetish man pricked each of our right arms, pressed the blood out ... and the black and white arms were mutually rubbed together."

In its simplest form, a blood pact involves a couple of pinpricked fingers and two friends becoming "blood brothers" (or sisters!), maybe in front of a blazing bonfire on a summer camping trip.

Blood pacts are an extreme way of showing devotion. It's not exactly something you'd want to try with your soccer team or your math class. In fact, thanks to our modern knowledge of blood-borne diseases, blood pacts aren't something that anyone wants to try. Not anymore.

In the past, though, people did find uses for these sorts of rites.

Street gangs, for example, have been known to use blood pacts or blood initiations. In the late 1990s, as the Los Angeles gang the Bloods expanded their realm to include New York City, the leaders told new recruits to attack random members of the public. The result? There were 135 "initiation-rite" slashings. And if the Bloods of Los Angeles were known for *spilling* blood, the Kenyan Mungiki gang was known for *drinking* it. Active in the late 1990s and revived in 2008, the group forced new members to drink blood as part of their initiation. There was plenty of blood-spilling as well, mostly in the streets of Nairobi.

The history of blood pacts and blood initiations extends back much further. In ancient Rome, members of the cult of Mithras celebrated the birth of the god and his sacrifice of the first bull. From the bull's blood, it was believed, came the earth's fertility, and the bread and wine that would feed humankind. To gain entrance into this cult, initiates would undergo seven tests of strength and endurance; they would be branded, exposed to extreme heat and cold, and possibly thrown across open pits. Finally, survivors were baptized in the blood of a bull.

BLOOD MAGIC

In 1791, the black slaves of Saint-Dominigue (now Haiti) were ready to revolt against their French rulers. But the leaders needed hundreds of thousands of slaves to take part, and they needed a way to inspire these people. They held a voodoo ceremony in which leaders drank the blood of a sacrificed pig. The rebellion succeeded, and the priestess who presided over the voodoo ceremony was named a goddess. She is honored today with ritual sacrifices of black pigs.

BLOOD FOR BLESSINGS

Blood links families. It can be used to tie friends—or gang members—together as if they're family. Now, what if people decide to *give* their blood for the same cause? They would be taking group action, in a way, through blood.

That's exactly what happens in northern India, where a number of religious sects promote blood donation. The leaders see this as a way to do good for fellow humans, and for their country. In 2005, one group donated enough blood to fill 67 bathtubs—in a single day. They earned themselves a place in that year's *Guinness World Records*.

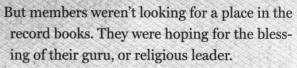

But members weren't looking for a place in the record books. They were hoping for the blessing of their guru, or religious leader.

They may have also wanted something more controversial: a way to help the Indian Army. Because these religious groups believe in non-violence, they are forbidden from participating directly in battles. But they're also very patriotic, and eager to support their country. One way for them to do so—at a safe and acceptable distance—is to provide blood for wounded soldiers. Across geographic distances, and across philosophical boundaries, the blood provides a way for the religious group and the soldiers to tie themselves to the same cause.

DEEP DIVISIONS

If sharing blood can replicate family bonds, or help vastly different people to participate in the same cause, the refusal to share blood can represent something far different. It can mean deep distrust, or even hatred.

In the late 1920s, Otto Reche co-founded the German Society for the Study of Blood Groups, trying to show a relationship between blood types, which had recently been discovered, and racial characteristics. He wanted to pinpoint the ultimate blond-and-blue-

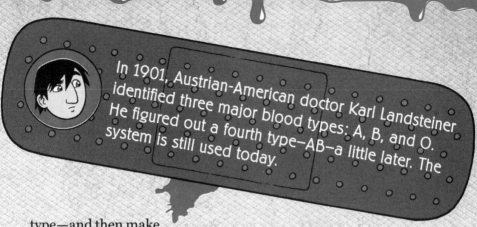

In 1901, Austrian-American doctor Karl Landsteiner identified three major blood types: A, B, and O. He figured out a fourth type—AB—a little later. The system is still used today.

type—and then make sure only this blood type populated Germany. After years of ridiculously flawed research, he decided that type A blood was best, and people with this blood type should resettle an Aryan Europe.

The big problem with his research was geography. If Otto tested a mostly blond village and found mostly type A blood, it was because of small-town intermarriage, not because of a relationship between fair skin and type A blood.

These distinctions didn't matter to Adolf Hitler and his fellow Nazis. The dictator was obsessed with creating a superior race and he had no problem using whatever he could to justify his actions. He wanted a nation of people with the "purest" blood. And that caused problems for a German doctor named Hans Serelman.

NO MORE
MR. TOUGH GUY

Criminals worry about infectious diseases, just like everyone else. In Hong Kong, organized crime groups known as triads used to hold initiation ceremonies in which everyone's blood was mixed in a single bowl and then slurped by each new member. Now, they've ditched the bowl. Recruits suck blood from their own fingers instead.

In 1935, Dr. Serelman donated his own blood to a patient, when no other blood donor could be found. The patient was saved. Rather than being rewarded for his heroic efforts, Dr. Serelman was punished, simply because the dedicated doctor was Jewish and so was assumed to have the wrong type of blood. The Nazis charged him with contaminating the blood of the pure German race, and sent him to a concentration camp.

This was just one example of the ongoing campaign to purify Germany's bloodlines. In 1935, Hitler signed the Law for the Protection of German Blood and German Honor, designed to ensure that fair-skinned Germans wouldn't intermarry with Jews or other non-Aryans.

When Hitler took power, there were 9000 Jewish doctors practicing in Germany. Five years later, there were fewer than 700. The rest were forced out of business, sent to concentration camps, or had fled the country.

Traditionally, the caste system in India was just as strict as Hitler's ideas about marriage. According to the system, everyone belonged to a certain caste, or social group. Priests belonged to one group, craftspeople to another, and warriors to another. People worked, lived, and married only within their castes. At one time, almost anyone in India would have said that caste was part of a person's blood. You were born into a caste, and the distinction flowed through your veins.

Then came the discovery of blood types. There was no specific scientific blood type for high-ranking priests, and no specific type for the manual laborers in the lowest caste. For activists who were fighting against the caste system—arguing that your choice of job or spouse should be *your* choice—blood types seemed like the ideal tool. If people of different castes could have the same blood type, and people of the same caste could have different blood types, then people clearly weren't born to live in a certain caste, the way they were born with their blood types. Right?

In parts of India, the debate continues. But blood banks are anonymous and make no caste distinctions. That means there are plenty of Brahmin (high caste) people walking around with lower-caste blood, and vice versa.

When doctors began performing blood transfusions in India, some people believed that donating blood would sap their strength. They believed this so strongly that they temporarily lost the use of their arms after giving blood . . . for psychological, not physical, reasons.

Harker's Personal Notes

All these blood ties. They're boggling my brain.

💀 What if some great-grandma of mine had carried hemophilia? Would I have been born?

💀 Queen Victoria knew there was a problem with her bloodlines. Was it okay for her to marry off her kids all over Europe?

💀 Are there still "blue bloods"? Does this country have families that hold lots of power, generation after generation?

💀 That oath. I've tied myself to these vampires, with actual blood. Has it changed the way I feel? Am I more loyal? Is blood powerful enough to bind me to this new family . . . forever?

CHAPTER 5
READING THE BLOOD

THE NOBEL PRIZE for Medicine goes to ... drum roll, please ... Dr. Karl Landsteiner, for discovering blood types, among other things! Kudos all around, wild applause, Facebook and the Twitterverse are abuzz!

Well, okay. Maybe there was no social media action. Karl made his discovery in 1901 and won the prize in 1930, long before the time of the Internet. Still, blood types were big news. Years before Otto Reche began his wacky research, scientists found that different types had unique ways of reacting to invaders such as germs or viruses—or a blood transfusion. With this knowledge, doctors could finally match blood donors to recipients, making transfusions much safer. They even saved lives.

There were other applications for blood typing, too. Way back at the turn of the century, Karl predicted that his techniques could be used in paternity cases, when a court was trying to decide whether or not a particular man was the father of a particular baby.

THE BIG SWITCH

sciencebook Profile

Karl Landsteiner
Just won the Nobel Prize! Woot! Woot!

Hometown:
Vienna, Austria

Birthday:
June 14, 1868

Interests:
Blood, Viruses, Classification Systems

n the 1800s, people would match babies with fathers by comparing eye color, head shape, or skin tone.

In 1930, two families took their newborn babies home from a Chicago hospital. Once home, though, they discovered something strange. The baby that went with the Watkins family wore a "Baby Bamberger" label, and the baby at home with the Bambergers wore a Watkins label.

Uh-oh.

Were the babies backwards, or the labels?

At first, the hospital suggested that the families keep the kids they had, wait for them to get older, and see which kid looked like which parents. The parents weren't too happy with that option.

The commissioner of health called in the experts: a criminologist, an anthropologist, a dermatologist, an ophthalmologist, a psychiatrist, an obstetrician, a podiatrist, and a pathologist. The majority of the experts, including the one using newfangled blood-type information, said the babies had been switched. A month after their birth, the children were returned to their proper families. Baby Watkins became Baby Bamberger, and vice versa.

HMMM... YES, YOU BOTH HAVE BROWN EYES. YOU'RE DEFINITELY THE FATHER.

BABY BLUES

Dr. Louis K. Diamond, a professor at Harvard Medical School, figured out something life-shattering (literally) in 1932. When a mother *without* a certain protein in her blood had a baby *with* the same protein, the baby was in danger. During birth, the two bloods would mix, and the mother's blood could attack the baby's blood, the way it would attack a virus or infection. For the baby, this could be fatal.

Even after Dr. Diamond's discovery, finding a treatment took years. Eventually, Dr. Diamond found a way to save babies with oh-so-tiny blood transfusions. Today, mothers at risk are injected with a special blood product, to change the way the blood's immune system reacts to the baby.

STAINED REPUTATIONS

Back in 1901, Karl Landsteiner predicted yet another use for blood type info—as evidence in murder investigations.

Imagine this: a man comes home to find his wife murdered. When the police arrive, they see a bloodstain on the husband's shirt. Aha! He's the murderer!

But the husband insists he's innocent. He says the bloodstain is from a nosebleed earlier that day.

Until the early 1900s, the husband's fate would have depended on whether or not the court believed him. And murder versus nosebleed . . . what would you believe?

Well, a case just like this one went to trial in Italy in the 1920s. Fortunately, Dr. Leone Lattes was there to help. He was an expert in blood and its role in legal cases. In 1915, he'd discovered a way to determine blood type from a dried bloodstain. He was able to prove that the shirt was spotted with the husband's own blood—the man was telling the truth about his nosebleed, and he was innocent.

The ability to determine the blood type of a dried-out smudge changed many more trials and murder cases ... and that was just the beginning. Since Leone's days, scientists have developed an arsenal of investigation techniques. And there's an entire field called forensics, or crime scene investigation— devoted to examining crimes to gather scientific evidence.

SPATTER POWER

Blood spatter is a technical term for the blood and gunk that spews out of a body when a violent death occurs. (And if that's enough to make your stomach feel queasy, you might want to skip this next section.)

The first guy to study blood spatter was a Polish scientist named Dr. Eduard Piotrowski, in the late 1800s. He showed how the size of blood drops, the direction of spatter, and the shape of the blood could reveal facts about a crime. For example, if someone is hit on one side of his head, blood will spray in the opposite direction.

HOW DID PIOTROWSKI LEARN ALL THIS STUFF?

HE EXPERIMENTED ON RABBITS.

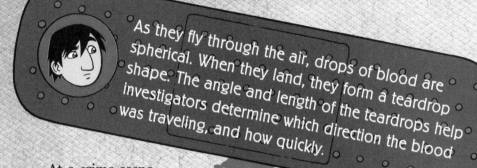

As they fly through the air, drops of blood are spherical. When they land, they form a teardrop shape. The angle and length of the teardrops help investigators determine which direction the blood was traveling, and how quickly.

At a crime scene where the blood spatter is all to the right of a dead body, the investigators can tell that the murderer was standing on the left.

Thankfully, scientists no longer use rabbits to study spatter. They do, however, visit crime scenes. There's a whole field of experts and analysts who specialize in "reading" blood. There's even an International Association of Bloodstain Pattern Analysts. These are scientists and police officers (about 800 of them, worldwide) who know how to tell the marks made by a bleeding vein from the spurts made by an artery. They know the difference between a blood transfer—an impression left by a bloody knife, for example— and a blood swipe made by the palm of a hand.

In a murder case, the experts examine the blood evidence to determine exactly how the victim was killed. They might even be able to tell what weapon was used, simply by scanning the drops left behind.

💀 Low-velocity spatter is a term used to describe big drops of blood. Maybe someone was hit on the head and blood slowly dripped to the floor, forming small pools.

💀 Medium-velocity spatter might be present if someone was repeatedly beaten or stabbed. It's basically medium-sized drops, created by blood that was moving at medium speed.

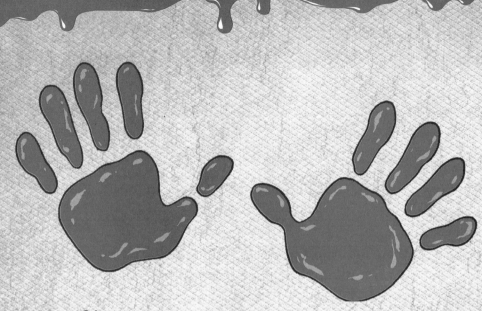

💀 High-velocity spatter comes from a gunshot wound, an explosion, or some other quick and violent force. The body was hit at great speed, which created a spray, or mist, of tiny droplets.

Experts also use special lights and chemicals to see bloodstains that are too faded or too small for the naked eye. Thanks to these techniques, investigators can detect traces of blood even after most of it has been washed down the sink. Or they can see residue on clothing—even if the clothes have gone through the washing machine.

If all of this sounds high tech, it is. But the ideas behind bloodstain analysis and crime scene investigation have been around for a long time.

💀 In Rome in 1100 CE, a blind man was accused of killing his mother. A lawyer named Quintilian examined the bloody handprints at the crime scene, found they didn't match the son's hands, and proved the son innocent.

💀 In 1813, a Spanish chemistry professor named Mathiew Orfila became the first to examine blood evidence using microscopes. He also developed tests to detect tiny amounts of blood.

In the 1887 novel *A Study in Scarlet*, Sherlock Holmes talks about a way to detect tiny, trace amounts of blood. Scientists at the time were working on chemical tests to do just that, but the methods hadn't yet been perfected.

In 1937, German scientist Walter Specht developed luminol, a chemical that makes blood glow blue. It's still used by investigators today.

Every year, there are new developments in forensics. A Swiss team recently found a way to use lasers and computer imaging to recreate the arc that drops of blood travel through the air, from victim to spatter. In the Netherlands, scientists have found a way to determine the age of a victim, using only a bloodstain.

Gross but true: flies eat blood. They walk around in crime scenes and mess with the clues. But today, labs can test for evidence found in blood—even after it's gone through a fly's digestive tract.

BIRTH OF THE CRIME LAB

Scotland Yard—officially known as the Metropolitan Police Service of London—has investigated serious crimes in England since 1829. In 1901, the organization began analyzing fingerprints. The first laboratory designed especially for processing this sort of police evidence opened in France in 1910. In the United States, a Los Angeles police chief created the country's first crime lab in 1924. The FBI opened its own version eight years later.

FUTURISTIC FORMULAE

Although the blood groups discovered by Karl Landsteiner are still recognized, scientists have now identified more than 30 distinct types within those basic groups. Each one carries its own antigens, microscopic substances that change the way a body's immune system reacts. Being able to recognize the subtle differences between types helps doctors practice better medicine, and helps the police with crime scene investigation.

Modern courts also accept DNA evidence, which can be drawn from blood or from any cellular material—a strand of hair, a scraping of skin, or a drop of saliva. DNA is a substance within the cells of every living creature. It carries the genetic instructions for the body. Your DNA tells your body whether to make red hair or brown, and whether your nose will be long or short. Because each person has unique DNA, samples can be used to identify criminals—or fathers.

Not only can scientists now determine exactly which parents belong to which child, they can tell which child belongs to which great-great-great-great grandfather. They've even identified the living descendants of Genghis Khan.

Every year, geneticists, biologists, and forensics experts make new discoveries. Steadily, the ability to "read" a person's blood is becoming more and more precise.

Harker's Personal Notes

Now I'm fully immersed in a world of blood. And it seems like everyone else is, too— vampire or human.

What if I was switched at the hospital at birth? (Now that would explain a few things!)

 I've been thinking about all the crime shows on TV. What draws all those fans?

If we can identify people so well, first by blood type and now by DNA analysis, how do we still sometimes send innocent people to jail?

CONCLUSION
A TASTE FOR BLOOD

"**IF IT BLEEDS, IT LEADS.**" That's a famous newspaper rule about putting gore and violence on the front page. Shock value draws more readers.

It also draws real-life viewers. Imagine there's a car accident on the highway. Commuters are delayed for hours as vehicles snake from the scene, bumper to bumper. But, wait. Cars aren't only backed up *behind* the accident. They're backed up on the other side of the road, too! Even though the accident doesn't directly affect them—even though there's a concrete divider between the lanes—drivers are slowing down to check out the action.

105

Why? Why do people "rubber neck" at car crashes? The emergency vehicles have arrived, there's nothing an average driver can do, and yet people still slow down, creating traffic havoc.

Violent crashes capture our attention, something that hasn't escaped the notice of entertainment experts. Movies such as *The Fast and the Furious* and *Dawn of the Dead* glamorize the thrill of the chase and the drama of the crash. In Toronto, TV producers promoted one show by staging a fake plane crash, complete with fake smoke. The stunt resulted in masses of 911 calls.

RATED M FOR ... MORE?

Meanwhile, experts endlessly debate the effects of violent video games. There's no question that games—like movies and television shows—are growing more realistic, more violent, and more bloody. At the same time, rates of violent crime in North America are actually dropping. So, do violent video games encourage youth violence? Or do they give young people an outlet for aggression? A safe way to let off steam?

No one knows the answer to those questions. Some studies say one thing and some say another. The debate is not new, either. More than 2000 years ago, people were asking the same questions

"Warning. The show you are about to watch may contain extreme violence. Viewer discretion is advised." A recent study found that warnings like this one make people more likely to watch the show.

about violence in the Roman Coliseum. Gladiators hacked and slashed each other. Blood spurted everywhere for the entertainment of the crowds. In one gore-fest, fighters slaughtered a thousand wild cats.

Some Romans said that all of this killing was abhorrent, unnatural, and immoral. Others said that the citizens had grown up in times of war. They craved blood, action, and excitement. Give them a few hours of Coliseum violence, and they wouldn't need to fight each other in the streets.

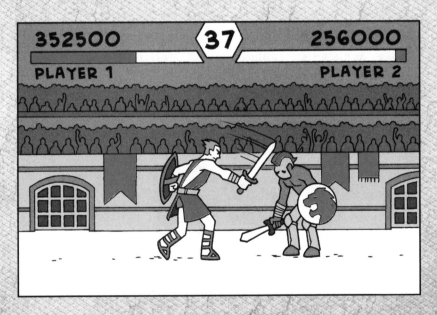

Eventually, Roman emperor Constantine put a damper on the gladiator games—not because he disapproved of the violence, but because he needed more fighters. Killing all those slaves and soldiers was draining his resources for war.

Meanwhile, the questions of violence as entertainment lived on—to be discussed while political prisoners faced the guillotine in France, or matadors taunted bulls in the arenas of Spain, or mixed martial arts competitors wrestled on blood-soaked mats.

HUNGRY FOR BLOOD

In the novel *The Hunger Games*, an ordinary teen named Katniss is pitted against other contestants in a life-and-death battle, all for the enjoyment of a reality TV audience. Thousands tune in to see the bloodshed. The situation is futuristic and extreme... but is it far-fetched?

BORN FOR BLOOD?

Humans evolved as predators. We hunted woolly mammoths and saber-toothed tigers and other humans until we claimed dominance at the top of the food chain. All that hunting and war-making left us with an ingrained need for violence. A craving for blood.

That's one theory. There are plenty more:

☠ Pain stimulates the nervous system, the same way pleasure does. A gory horror film is like a chocolate ice-cream cone on a hot day—a delicious shiver down the spine.

☠ In modern times, everyday life has become a boring routine of bed, breakfast, work or school, and back to bed. A bit of violence wakes us up.

AS THE WORLD *SPINS*

In a crisis, most people spring into action . . . others pass out. Some scientists believe that people faint at the sight of blood because thousands of years ago, "playing dead" in a dangerous situation may have fooled enemy attackers. Today, anyone determined to overcome this phobic fainting can visit a psychologist for treatment.

We rarely talk about death. Watching media violence is a way to consider our own feelings about the end of life—and experience the thrill of survival.

There are no right answers to questions about violence in society. All we can do—the next time we turn our heads at a car accident, or look to see who's fighting on the school playground—is ask ourselves why. Why do we look? What draws us to the sight of blood?

Once, blood was a part of sacred rituals. It was a symbol of the soul, believed to carry our characteristics and our thoughts. It tied us to our families, and bound us to our gods. In the 21st century, has blood retained its sacred side? Or is it simply a cheap video-game thrill for a dull Saturday afternoon?

It's possible that the very fact that blood still thrills us—still stops us, shocks us, and scares us—is a sign that it retains some of its strange power. In a world where the average 18-year-old has witnessed thousands of staged TV murders, blood is still something real.

It's still a symbol of life, and a sign of death.

FURTHER READING

Armentrout, David and Patricia. *Blood Suckers*. Vero Beach, FL: Rourke Publishing, 2010.

Bjorklund, Ruth. *Circulatory System*. New York: Marshall Cavendish Benchmark, 2009.

Bunson, Matthew. *The Vampire Encyclopedia*. New York: Gramercy, 2000.

Deary, Terry. *Horrible Histories: Amazing Aztecs*. New York: Scholastic, 2010.

Eyewitness Forensic Science. London: Dorling Kindersley, 2008.

Green, Jen. *Aztecs*. New York: PowerKids Press, 2009.

Guiley, Rosemary. *Vampires*. New York: Chelsea House Publishers, 2008.

Kottler, Jeffrey A. *The Lust for Blood*. Amherst, NY: Prometheus Books, 2010.

Lew, Kristi. *Clot and Scab*. Minneapolis: Lerner Publishing, 2009.

Senior, Kathryn. *You Wouldn't Want To Be Sick in the 16th Century!* New York: Franklin Watts, 2002.

Stewart, Gail B. *Forensics*. Detroit: KidHaven Press, 2007.

SELECTED SOURCES

Akin, Louis L. "Blood Spatter Interpretation at Crime and Accident Scenes." *FBI Law Enforcement Bulletin*. Feb. 2005: 22–24.

Bartlett, Wayne, and Flavia Idriceanu. *Legends of Blood*. Westport, CT: Praeger, 2005.

"Blood Initiation." From the website of *National Geographic News*. http://video.nationalgeographic.com/video/player/places/regions-places/australia-and-oceania/newguinea-bloodinitiation-pp.html. Accessed April 30, 2011.

Bower, B. "Ritual Clues Flow from Prehistoric Blood." *Science News*. Dec. 23, 1989: 405.

Bower, Bruce. "Blood and Sacrifice." *Science News*. June 7, 1986: 360–62.

——. "Contagious Thoughts." Science News. Aug. 31, 1991: 138.

Brunaux, Jean-Louis. "Gallic Blood Rites." *Archaeology*. March/April 2001: 54.

Buckley, Thomas, and Alma Gottlieb. *Blood Magic*. Berkeley: University of California Press, 1988.

Bushman, Brad J. "Effects of Warning and Information Labels on Attraction to Television Violence in Viewers of Different Ages." *Journal of Applied Social Psychology*. Sept. 2006: 2073–78.

Camporesi, Piero. *Juice of Life*. New York: Continuum, 1995.

Childress, Sarah, and Sammy Kagwanja. "Kenyan Gang Revives amid Political Disarray." *Wall Street Journal—Eastern Edition*. May 1, 2008: A12.

Copeman, Jacob. "Violence, Non-Violence, and Blood Donation in India." *Journal of the Royal Anthropological Institute*. June 2008: 278–96.

Cox, Timothy M., et al. "King George III and Porphyria." *Lancet*. July 23, 2005: 332–35.

Daniels, Geoff, and Marion E. Reid. "Blood Groups: The Past 50 Years." *Transfusion*. Feb. 2010: 281–89.

Englert, Rod, with Kathy Passero. *Blood Secrets*. New York: St. Martin's Press, 2010.

Giusti, G.V. "Leone Lattes: Italy's Pioneer in Forensic Serology." *The American Journal of Forensic Medicine and Pathology*. March 1982: 79–82.

Hayes, Bill. *Five Quarts*. New York: Ballantine Books, 2005.

"The History of Hemophilia." From the website of the Canadian Hemophilia Society. http://www.hemophilia.ca/en/bleeding-disorders/hemophilia-a-and-b/the-history-of-hemophilia/. Accessed June 13, 2011.

Hofstadter, Dan. "The Aztecs: Blood and Glory." *Smithsonian*. Jan. 2005: 76–85.

Hutson, Matthew. "Rite of Way." *Psychology Today*. May/June 2008.

Inman, Keith, and Norah Rudin. *Principles and Practice of Criminalistics*. Boca Raton, FL: CRC Press, 2000.

Kearney, Caitlin. "Blood Simple." *Popular Science*. April 2001: 38.

Kocieniewski, David. "Youth Gangs from West Coast Become Entrenched in New York." *New York Times*. Aug. 28, 1997:1.

Kottler, Jeffrey A. *Lust for Blood*. Amherst, NY: Prometheus Books, 2011.

Lewis, Brenda Ralph. "For Kith and Kin." *British Heritage*. Nov. 2006: 42–45.

"Medicine: Baby Fight." From the website *Time*. http://www.time.com/time/magazine/article/0,9171,740025,00.html. Accessed June 20, 2011.

Pogue, Tiffany D. "Bois Caiman." *Encyclopedia of African Religion*. Thousand Oaks, CA: Sage Publications, 2009.

Potts, D.M., and W.T.W. Potts. *Queen Victoria's Gene*. Phoenix Mill, UK: Alan Sutton, 1995.

Potts, W.T.W. "Royal Haemophilia." *Journal of Biological Education*, v. 30. 1996: 207–17.

Powell, Julie. "The Trouble with Blood." *Archaeology*. Nov./Dec. 2004: 34.

Rosen, Jeff. "Blood Ritual." *New Republic*. Nov. 2, 1992: 9–10.

"Scarification." From the website of *National Geographic News*. http://news.nationalgeographic.com/news/2004/07/0728_040728_tvtabooscars_2.html. Accessed April 30, 2011.

Simon, John S. "Kaniyan: Ritual Performers of Tamil Nadu, South India." *Asian Ethnology*. Spring 2008: 123–35.

Starr, Douglas. *Blood*. New York: Alfred A. Knopf, 1998.

Van der Kiste, John. *Queen Victoria's Children*. Phoenix Mill, UK: Sutton, 2003.

Van Gelder, Lawrence. "Arts, Briefly." *New York Times*. Dec. 16, 2004: 2.

Watkins, Nancy. "Baby I'm yours—I think." From the website of the *Chicago Tribune*. http://articles.chicagotribune.com/2004-06-27/features/0406270450_1_babies-blood-tests-englewood-hospital. Accessed June 20, 2011.

INDEX

Africa 35, 39, 42, 48, 58, 64, 80, 82
AIDS 56, 79
Albania 59
antigens 101
Arctic 48, 50
arteries 4, 20, 70, 96
Arthur (king of the Britons) 55
Aryan 85, 86
Asante people 39, 42
Asia 47, 54
Australia 13, 43
Austria 62, 73
Aztecs 15–16, 21, 29

Bamberger baby 92–93
Bathory, Elizabeth 61–62
Beng people 39
Bhutan 73
Bible 21, 22, 52
bile 5, 9
black pudding 47, 51
blodplättar 51
blood
  banks 71–72, 88
  brothers 1, 79–80
  cubes 48, 50
  donation 71, 83–84, 91;
    see also blood banks

blood (cont.)
  feud 68
  pacts 1, 79–80, 82, 89
  pancakes 51
  rites 1, 16, 18, 21, 26,
    31–42, 79, 80
  sausage 47, 51
  spatter 1, 95–98
  ties 1, 9, 67–69, 72,
    79–84, 89, 108
  tofu 48
  transfusions 64, 70–72,
    88, 91–92, 93
  types 2, 9, 84–85, 88,
    91–92, 93, 101, 103
  wings 36
bloodletting 1, 5–7
bloodlust 29
Bloods, the 82
blue bloods 1, 78, 89
body piercing 35
Brahmin 88
brain 9, 53, 69
Brazil 58
Britain 51, 55, 63, 73,
  74–75
Buckingham Palace 72
Buffy the Vampire Slayer
  62

California 24
Canada 48, 51
car accidents 9, 105–6
castes 88
Castile 78
Catholic Church 23, 24,
  26, 58
Central America 13
Chicago 92
Christianity 21, 22–23, 55
circulatory system 3–4, 9,
  53, 70
circumcision 38, 76
clans 68–69
clotting factors 76
Coliseum 57, 58, 107
coming-of-age ceremo-
  nies 31–42, 44–45
Commonwealth 72
Communion 22–23
computer imaging 100
Constantine (emperor of
  Rome) 108
cow's blood 48, 70, 82
creation myths 10
Crete 59
crime scene investiga-
  tion. See forensics
crocodiles 33
crucifixion 23

cultural views on blood 10, 36, 38–44, 51
   as rooted in the body 10
culture 1, 9; *see also* myths, religion
"cutters" 33

Dawn of the Dead 106
death 2, 11, 18, 20, 21, 22, 43, 59, 62, 64, 71, 95, 108, 110
Denis, Jean-Baptiste 70–71
Diamond, Dr. Louis K. 93
dinuguan 50
DNA 102, 103
Dracula 63, 65
drinking blood 55–59, 63, 64
duck's blood 48, 50

eating blood 1, 9, 47–52, 54, 55, 57–59, 61, 65
   black pudding 47
   blodplättar 51
   blood sausage 47, 51
   blood tofu 48
   dinuguan 50
   halal food 52
   kosher food 52
   sanguinaccio 47
   seal's blood 48
   tiet canh 50
   yak blood cubes 48
Edward, Prince 77
Egypt 3, 5, 13, 22, 58
England 7, 72, 73, 74, 101; *see also* Britain
Ethiopia 34

Europe 5, 6, 13, 18, 47, 53, 54, 55, 56, 62, 63, 71, 73, 74, 75, 76, 77, 79, 85
executions 57

Fast and the Furious, The 106
FBI 101
"fetishes" 43
Filipino people 50
fingerprints 101
flies 100
Florida 26
forensics 94–102
Founding of the Congo Free State, The 80
France 7, 18, 42, 73, 108
Fulani people 35

Galen, Claudius 3, 7, 69–70
gangs 82, 83, 86
Gauls 18–19, 21
genetics 67, 74, 102; *see also* blood types
Genghis Khan 102
George III (king of England) 75
German Society for the Study of Blood Groups 84–85
Germany 74, 84–85, 86
germs 7
Ghana 39, 42
gladiators 3, 57, 107–8
God 9, 21, 22, 23, 39, 54, 56
gods 10, 13, 14, 15, 16, 18, 19, 20, 22, 28, 82, 110
Greece 5, 68

guillotine 108
Guinness World Records 83
Gutenberg 6

Haiti 83
halal food 52
Harvey, William 4, 5
heart 2, 3, 4, 10, 16, 20, 29, 53, 59, 69
hemophilia 74–77, 89
hepatitis C 79
Hitler, Adolf 85–86, 88
Holmes, Sherlock 100
Holy Grail 55–56
Hong Kong 86
Huehueteotl 16
Huitzilopochtli 16
humors 5
Hungary 61–62
Hunger Games, The 108
Hussein, Imam 27

imborivungu 44
immune system 93, 101
India 21, 39, 58, 59, 83–84, 88
Indonesia 39
initiations 31–42, 44–45, 82
International Association of Bloodstain Pattern Analysts 96
Interview with the Vampire 62
Inuit people 48
Islam 27–28, 52
Israelites 22, 52
Italy 24, 94
Ivory Coast 39, 64

Jackman, Hugh 62
Japan 24, 26, 59, 73
Jesus 22, 23, 55, 56
Jewish beliefs 22, 52, 76
Jews 21, 78, 86
Jordan 73
jump wings 36

Kaniyan people 21–22
Karo tribe 34
Kenya 82
Knights of the Round Table 55
kosher food 52
Kwakiutl people 43

lamb's blood 22
lampreys 54
Landsteiner, Karl 85, 91–92, 94, 101
Last Supper 55
Lattes, Dr. Leone 94–95
Law for the Protection of German Blood and German Honor 86
law of contagion 56–58, 65
Lebanon 27
leeches 7, 54
Leopold, Prince 75, 77
leprosy 58
Lestat 62
lion hunting 35–36
liver 2, 4, 43, 69
Lodur 10
Los Angeles 82, 101
luminol 100
lungs 3, 9

Maasai people 35–36, 48
Madonna. See Virgin Mary

Mae Enga people 42
Maria Theresa (empress of Austria) 62
matadors 108
Matsusa people 31–32, 33
Maya people 14–15
menstrual blood 42–44, 51
menstruation 38–42, 76
Mesopotamia 50
Metropolitan Police Service of London 101
Mexico 13, 15, 54, 59; see also Aztecs; Maya people
Meyer, Stephenie 9
microscopes 98
Middle Ages 57
Middle East 5, 6
miracles 24–26
Mithras 82
mixed martial arts 108
monarchies 72–75, 77, 79
Mongolia 50
Montenegro 68–69
Moors 78
morganatic blood 73
Morocco 73
mosquitoes 54
Mungiki gang 82
muscles 9
Muslim 27–28, 39
myths 9, 10–11

Nairobi 82
Nazis 86
Netherlands 100
New York City 82
Nigeria 44
Noah 21
Nobel, Alfred 6

Nobel Prize 91
Norse mythology 10
North America 6, 13, 39, 43, 47, 78, 106
Norway 73

ochre 43
offerings 13, 14, 22, 28, 29
Ontario 51
Orfila, Mathiew 98

Papua New Guinea 31–33, 42
parachutist badge 36
Passover 22
Pasteur, Louis 7
paternity 92, 102
Percival 55
pharaohs 6, 58
phlegm 5
pig's blood 48, 83
Piotrowski, Dr. Eduard 95
Pliny the Elder 43
poison 42, 43
Polynesia 35
porphyria 63, 74, 75
Portugal 10, 39
potions 42
Presbyterian Church 23
protein 48, 93
puberty 38
Pueblo people 39
pus 7

Quebec 51
Quintilian 98
Qur'an 52

Reche, Otto 84–85, 91
Red Cross 64

relics 58
religion 1, 9, 13–29, 78, 83–84, 110
  Aztec 15–16
  Catholic 23–26
  Christian 21, 22–23, 55, 78
  and eating blood 52, 54
  Gaul 18–19
  Islam 27–28, 52
  Jewish 21, 22, 52, 76
  Kaniyan 21–22
  Maya 13–15
  Santeria 26
  Shiite 27–28
Rice, Anne 62
rites 1, 2, 16, 18, 21, 26, 43, 79, 80
  of passage 31–42, 44–45
Roman Catholic Church. *See* Catholic Church
Rome 3, 5, 24, 53, 57, 58, 82, 98, 107–8
roosters 26
royal blood 72–73
Russia 58, 74, 75
Russian Revolution 77

sacrifice 1, 13–16, 18–19, 21–23, 43, 54
  animal 13, 18, 22, 26, 28, 29, 82, 83
  human 13, 15–16, 18–19, 28, 44
Saint-Dominigue. *See* Haiti
sangre azul 78
sanguinaccio 47
Santeria 26
scarring 33, 34

Scotland 68
Scotland Yard 101
seal's blood 48
Sepik River 33
Serelman, Hans 85–86
Servetus, Michael 4
Shiite Muslims 27–28
Sierra Leone 39
soul 19, 20–21, 54, 59, 110
South America 47, 54
Soviet Union 77
Spain 47, 61, 73, 75, 78, 98, 108
Spanish Civil War 77
Specht, Walter 100
Stanley, Henry Morton 80
Stoker, Bram 63
Study in Scarlet, A 100
Sudalai 21–22
superstitions 56, 62, 70
Sweden 51
Sweeney Todd 48
symbols 9, 10, 11, 22, 23, 28, 33, 34, 42, 43, 44, 55, 68, 79, 110

taboos 2
Talmud 76
Tanganyikan people 64
tattoos 35
Tenochtitlan 15
Teresa, Mother 58
Tezcatlipoca 16
Thailand 73
Tibet 10, 48, 50
tiet canh 50
Tiv people 44
Toronto 106
Transylvania 58, 63
triads 86

Turkey 3, 18, 39
Tuscany 47
Twilight series 9, 58, 65

United States 36, 39, 42, 101
University of Connecticut 36
U.S. Armed Forces 36

vampire bats 54
Vampire Chronicles 62
vampire moths 54
vampires 1, 9, 58–59, 62–65, 75
Van Helsing 62
veins 1, 7, 20, 28, 70, 73, 76, 78, 88, 96
Victoria (queen of England) 74–75, 77, 79, 89
Vietnam 50
violence 106–10
  in video games 106, 110
Virgil 21
Virgin Mary 23–26
voodoo 83

war 15, 16, 36, 64, 67, 77, 107, 108, 109
Watkins baby 92–93
William, Prince 72–73
World War II 64
Wright, Almroth 76

yak blood cubes 48

Zambia 39

ABOUT THE AUTHOR

In situations involving blood, **TANYA LLOYD KYI** is rather useless. She's been known to pass out at the sight of needles. She closes her eyes during violent movie scenes. And during a crisis, she's usually the one wildly flapping her arms in a completely unhelpful manner. Fortunately, she didn't faint while writing this book (at least, not often), and even managed to look calmly at most of the illustrations. Tanya's the author of more than a dozen other books for young readers, including *The Lowdown on Denim* and the *50 Questions* series. She lives with her family in Vancouver, BC.

ABOUT THE ILLUSTRATOR

STEVE ROLSTON has been telling stories in the comic book medium for the past decade and has illustrated a range of genres, from the spy series *Queen & Country* to the punk rock comedy *Pounded*, from the teen drama *Emiko Superstar* to the supernatural thriller *Ghost Projekt*. His comic book work has earned an Eisner Award and a Cybils Award, as well as a couple of Shuster Award nominations.

Beyond comics, he also provided illustrations for the Annick Press book *The Great Motion Mission: A Surprising Story of Physics in Everyday Life*, written by Cora Lee. Steve lives in Vancouver, BC.

OTHER GREAT NONFICTION FROM ANNICK

ROYAL MURDER:
THE DEADLY INTRIGUE OF TEN SOVEREIGNS
BY ELIZABETH MACLEOD

"Audiences in grades five and up will love hearing these gory, intriguing tales."
—*School Library Journal*

Lots of people would kill to wear a crown, and royal history's got the bloodstains to prove it. Being king or queen is a dangerous job, and these thrilling stories of history's most infamous murdered and murdering sovereigns provide the bloody evidence.

BLOODY MOMENTS: HIGHLIGHTS FROM THE
ASTONISHING HISTORY OF MEDICINE
BY GAEL JENNINGS
ILLUSTRATED BY ROLAND HARVEY

"...a fascinating collection...the facts are undeniably compelling..."
—*School Library Journal*

Intriguing, funny, and totally gross: this quirkily illustrated history of medicine travels from the time before antibiotics to the future of cloning, taking in everything from plagues to nose transplants along the germ-infested path.